AF316678

Receiving Your Healing

How to prevail over life most difficult moments and live a life free from guilt, hurt, and bondage

Unleash unforgettable pain and manifest healing in your life through faith

Mianca Wright

Contents

Part 3: Manifest Healing

Introduction

It was in that very moment, coldly laid out, dreadfully crying, and defeated where I realized I was at my lowest. I was in an unusually gloomy and awful place feeling hopeless. I replayed every bad memory of my life in my head over and over again. I sorrowfully whispered to myself that not being here would be better for me.

With tears in my ears, I turned and looked at my beautiful daughter, peacefully sleeping and recognized she needed me. I needed to be firm and win for her. I built up my determination and said I would prevail. I am bent, but not broken. The road to receiving my healing starts now!

To my wonderful daughter, Nashiy, you are amazing! You will forever be my greatest success and the driving force behind my excellence. Mommy loves you to the moon and back, Baby Girl!

Preface

It took me forever and a day to put this short book together. I had to suck it up and just push it out to the world in the rawest and realist way possible. I had to face my fears on a whole new level. During this process, I had to take accountability for my actions, share some dark secrets that I had never imagined I would repeat and come to terms with some brutal truths. I had to be fearless. Being fearless meant letting down my guard, holding my head high, and being honest with myself and the world.

The truth is that at a point in time, I lived life as if I had it all together. I lived as if I never knew or heard of a hard life in the history of all my days. Nevertheless, this is far from the truth. I was hiding something. The fact of the matter is that we all have something profound hidden inside. Things unspeakable – things we want to forget – things we wish never happened – things we just cannot let go or get over. These examples all defined me. I was trying to appear rock-solid on the outside, yet troubled on the inside.

I was hurt, I was scared, I was confused, and I had no outlet that I genuinely connected with to express myself or understanding of healing. I didn't understand how to mend the most valuable and precious existence; I'll ever know – myself. I wanted so desperately to break free from the bondage. I wanted to throw my whole life away and had hoped that the spirit world would allow me to come back and start all over again with a new life. But this wasn't a game. I had to get serious. I needed to recognize that I'm significant and can receive healing just like anybody else. I had to reaffirm my value and rebuild up my worth that I allowed the world to tear down. It was time to manifest healing in my life

I hope that while reading this book, you are encouraged to elevate your thoughts concerning yourself. I inspire you to get honest with yourself and get set on the right path to healing. I want you to love yourself, love your family, dearest friends, and, ultimately, love God first and foremost. Not because I'm saying you should love God, but because He loves you too. I want you to know that even in your most difficult moments, God loves you because God is love. There's nothing you can do so severely to separate you from His love.

I wrote this book for people like you and for people like me who have been dealt a bad hand in life. God will come through in your darkest moments to prepare you for an even better experience. You were bent, but not broken. The road to your healing starts now, and it's time to manifest it.

Part 1: In the Beginning

He heals the brokenhearted and binds up their wounds.

~Psalms 147:3

Chapter 1

No Rest for the Weary

Many times, throughout life, we find ourselves lost, hurt, broken, abused, humiliated, or haunted by experience prolonged trauma. Life has a way of knocking us down time and time again and can turn a kind soul bitter or a pure heart black. This narrative doesn't have to be the outcome for you, however.

I suffered a great deal throughout my life. Some things I experienced were entirely out of my control, and other situations were a direct result of my actions. The horrible events in my life left me plagued with dark and sad thoughts. I repeatedly tried to work things out on my own, only to find myself coming up short and missing a piece of my complete healing puzzle every time.

Take Your Life Back

I declared that I would not be a victim or product of my past, nor to the guilt that came from my bad choices. I will be victorious! God has a plan and purpose for us all, and it's His will we live healthy and happy lives. Since you have decided to grab this book, I already know that your options are limited, and you are searching for something new. To discover it, you must turn from your typical perspective and thinking.

God Loves You

It doesn't matter what kind of lifestyle you live; God loves you. It doesn't matter how dark your past is; God loves you. It doesn't matter how you look; God loves you. It doesn't matter how much or little money you have; God loves you. Healing stands available to all of us, and God wants us to receive it! I invite you into my life, and I want to share my story with you to see how God set me free from things that have damaged me and left me feeling undeserving and shameful. God did it for me, and he can do it for you.

You must decide within your heart that you no longer want things to remain the way they are and release your hurt. Whether it's in your mind, your heart, your feelings, or your body – God got it. Confess healing with your mouth today. I had to go through this same process, through-out my life, and God placed it on my heart to share my testimony with others to be set free. We are all different and have suffered in many ways, but the process of healing is available for us all.

Chapter 2
Where It All Started

I grew up on the east side of Detroit, Michigan, in a very impoverished neighborhood where the crime was high, and drugs ran rapid. My mother was fifteen, still in high school when she gave birth to me. My mother and father had a rocky relationship during my early childhood. When I was three years old, my first brother was born. I was excited when he was born. I thought him to be my baby because of how close we grew over the years. Growing up, we always stuck together, no matter what. The trials we experienced in life required us to hold close together, and we made sure to do so.

As a child, I thought myself to be very peculiar and different. I didn't fit in with other kids. I was super smart; however, that didn't make me more or less satisfied with what I looked at in the mirror. I compared myself to other kids because I wasn't happy as a kid with how I looked. I dressed differently, had super, thick kinks, and didn't think highly of myself. I rarely had real friends in life and was considered the odd-ball often. Due to my lack of self-esteem and strange demeanor, I was out-casted. I was the weird kid in my neighborhood, and this followed me well into high school. This small thinking of myself fashioned the foundation to my self-esteem issues.

Not only did I suffer a great deal with self-esteem issues, but I also underwent many battles as a child that no child should ever have to face. I got ganged raped, went to foster care, was physically and emotionally abused, admitted into a psychiatric hospital as a child, and many other horrible things that struck me deep within the heart and made life unbearable to go through. Dealing with these types of battles can do only two things to a person. These battles can either break you down or minister to in building you up to face life differently.

For a while, my life battles tried to break me down. However, when I realized that I didn't have to be that product to my past that was to be destined for me, I got up, and I chose to heal. I also decided to build up others facing unbearable battles, too, just as I did to do the same.

In My Neighborhood

We lived in the ghetto, better known as "The Hood." Detroit is primarily known as Motown or Motor City. Even though my birth city had fancy labels and known to manufacture many high-end vehicles, it didn't improve or decrease the level of stress many families endured. Violence, gang-banging, and drugs ran rampant and sold as if it was needed like water in my neighborhood.

The men in my neighborhood were stone-cold gangsters or OGs and by no means hesitated to hit or beat on their women. Physical abuse was very prevalent. It didn't matter if you were a woman, man, or child; you better had known how to fight to live in my neighborhood. You could get into a fight any day with anyone for any reason. That was just the way we lived.

Your house could get broken into at any time, and your car could get stolen at any time too. People always were getting shot at and killed in our hood. Violence was all we knew because this was all we saw and what was in front of us. Poverty, hostility, and struggling to survive was our everyday life. Molestation and rape was a terrible epidemic many teenage girls experienced as well in our neighborhood. Numerous young girls had to suffer rape in silence because it was always an awful kept secret within families and turned a blind eye.

Every other household on my street relied on welfare, Focus Hope, WIC, and any other government assistance programs to feed their families. My mother and I lived with my great grand-granny when I was born, and it was at most, seven to eight individuals residing within her home at a time and sometimes more. Her house was the house of refuge, meaning that whenever life hit hard, and someone was without a place to stay, my great grand-granny house was the place to go. You can only imagine how hard it was to feed so many people with limited resources and income.

Rest in Peace

I loved my great grand-granny, also known as Mrs. Gardner, so much. She was the matriarch in our family and tried her hardest to keep us all together. She had a total of ten children and was initially born within the deep south in Birmingham, Alabama. Her mother, Mommy Tommy, was bought out of slavery and married at fifteen to a free man, better known as my great-great-grandfather,

Sandy Smith. They made the big decision to transition up north to Michigan, around the late 1930s.

My great-granny was smart, a praying warrior, loving, and nurturing. She was very wise and trustworthy – just an amazing woman and well respected. She used to speak at events to enlighten and encourage her community back-in-the-day as well. She also had a side that you didn't want to witness if you tried to cross her. It was nothing for her to turn up on anyone if they deserved it. She was not the type to be fooled or played.

I'll always remember my great-granny phenomenal cooking. My great-granny grew a garden in the backyard at a point in time too. When I was younger, I used to watch my great-granny get up early and take the jitney to the grocery store and come back with bags and bags of food for the household. She had no problem with providing plates to eat to other families in our neighborhood who needed it. She always did what she could for us and tried her best to take care of her family. You didn't have to be family by blood because my great-granny made anyone family by her love. Many people admired her, and her legacy and love will forever live-on.

Tragically, in the summer of July 4, 1998, she was brutally murdered in her own home. The murder went unsolved, and no suspects found. She was 68 when she went home to glory and taken from us. I was eight years old and could not attend her funeral. Due to events out of my control, I could not be there to give her one last hug and say goodbye for the last time. Not being able to attend my great-granny funeral hurt me significantly. I cried and was shattered by this for a long time.

I wanted my great grandmother to know that I loved her so much, and I wanted to thank her for advocating my existence into this world. She was so strong and did so much for her family and others. Life was hard for us, but she made sure everyone was loved and cared for in the best way she possibly could. Rest peacefully, my Loving Angel. I hope I've made you proud.

Chapter 3

Not For Me

Growing up in my neighborhood was taxing to my emotional health and not to mention, dangerous. Childhood, for me, wasn't peaceful nor pleasant. The lifestyle I lived had a negative affect on me, and as I grew into a teenager and adult, life tried to bankrupt me even more. There were limited examples of wholeness, and I wanted so desperately just to feel safe, secure and heard. But, since I didn't have what I desperately wanted, my perception of family, friends, and being an innocent little girl got ruined. I knew nothing else other than what was in front of me – brokenness.

The type of lifestyle I was born into can make you do only two things, be better and make it out or be a statistic. For me, even as a child, I understood this wasn't a healthy lifestyle or that I didn't want to be another statistic. There had to be more to life. I suffered so much. I always asked God, "Why did I have to be born into this lifestyle?" I was so young, yet I still comprehended that children should not live or feel emptiness so strongly the way I did.

It's Was Time

It came a time where I decided that the pain from my past would not affect me in my future, nor my present. It doesn't matter what you may have experienced growing up; you too can recover. You might have had an even more jagged life growing up than I did. Guess what – that doesn't matter. You might think after all this time, you're stuck and subjected to the cycle of mental and emotional scarring from your past, but you're not. Healing is the key. You have to decide today that you will leave your history behind and look towards a brighter future. Begin to set your mind up for healing and that you will not become a product to your past, but overcome it!

God Got You

If the pain from your past is so troublesome that you can't even repeat it, God got you! It doesn't matter if the doctor gave you a shocking medical report; God got you! Heartbreak, anxiety, addiction, or any other mountain standing before you inhibiting your breakthrough, God got you!

All it takes is having faith as small as a muster seed, and you can move mountains. A mustered is as tiny as a pinpoint tip, and God said that's all we need to move mountains. I am here to give you a guide on how I did it and how you can do it too.

By the grace of God, I am here to share my story with the world today – boldly and free from shame. I made it. Now, looking back on my earlier years, the struggle made me who I am. The hard life I had is the very reason I am a writer today. I encourage the healing process to everyone. Heal and be set free.

Chapter 4
My Family Tree

I describe my mother as being a robust flower or a modern-day Lara Croft. Lara Croft is the extraordinary character and superhero from the game Tomb Raider that I have forever loved since a child. Lara Croft is heroic, intelligent, beautiful, and a straight beast. I compare her to my mom. My mom will always be my shero! She's smart as a whip and has a balanced amount of femininity and dominance stitched within her personality. Along with being graceful, gifted, and all that jazz, she is all types of charismatic too. I always said that I got my charm and book smarts from her.

My mother also has an unmatched drive for excellence and possesses a vast amount of wisdom that I have never quite seen in anyone else. While caring for a child - me, she pushed herself to graduate early from high school at the age of 16, with honors. I cannot fathom the amount of grit and perseverance she needed to encompass to achieve this hard accomplishment. How amazing! Now, that is what I call a superhero.

I know for a fact that being a teenage mother wasn't easy. The added stress from a baby while maintaining exemplary grades is not a simple task at all. My mother pushed. She kept going. Things were tough, but she didn't give up. Considering the neighborhood that my mother got raised in and the type of standard of living that surrounded us, I honestly can say that she did well for herself and me. Her courage to keep striving for more and not settle the way she did is admirable.

I always look to my mother for strength. I use her as an example of how to live life modestly and gracefully. My early upbringing was rough; however, I knew that my mother, without a doubt, loved me and, as a teenager, did her very best. I will always respect her bravery and admiration for her children. I love you so much, mom, and if I haven't said it enough, thanks for all that you've done for me.

My Father

My father is hard to the core but soft as a teddy bear on the inside. He is all work and little play. Reliable and dedicated are the words I use to describe him. He is a hard worker and has never been lazy. My father's work ethic is without comparison. He has no trouble working hard for his family and for the things he desires in life. He always dresses to impress and can put an outstanding outfit together on any budget. His style always amazed me, even to this day. I get my hustle and fashionista swag from him. My parents have blessed me with a beautiful mix of gifts that have served me very well.

My father was the oldest out of four siblings, and he needed to be a hard worker and the most dependable. With being a hard worker, you can sometimes be hard on yourself. I always marveled at the way he handled this burden. When expected to have it all together and is the go-to person all the time, I can imagine that load getting heavier and heavier over time.

As I matured into an adult, I rationalized my father's decisions. I understood the reason behind the choices he made. Sometimes, you need a break, a break away from everything. A break away from burdens and a break away from being the go-to person all the time. Most importantly, a break from sustaining other people burdens, too. I know that my father loves me, and my very existence gives him life. I will forever love you, dad. In life, you have several aunts, uncles, cousins, and friends, but blessed with only one mother and one father. Honor them forever, no matter what.

My Brothers

Let me start by saying that I am the only girl amongst five brothers, which makes six of us total, but not all from the same batch. I am the second oldest out of the bunch. I have two stepbrothers, two half brothers, and one brother whom I share the same mother and father.

The word half brother or sister means you share only one parent with your siblings, either mother or father. However, I don't like to describe my brothers in that way. I consider them all to be family. Conversely, as complex as my genealogy is, I have a continuous relationship with only two of my brothers.

My brother, with whom I share the same mother and father and have a continuous relationship with, was my best friend. We are three years apart and stuck together the majority of our childhood. My baby brother, with whom I also have a constant relationship with, is seventeen years younger than me. That's a big jump, right? I won't go on to mention him much as he's so much younger than me.

Nevertheless, I will state that he's incredible and a little boy genius. I love you, Baby Brother!

I Am My Brother's Keeper

Together, in the past, my brother, also my best friend, did what we had to do to survive when life hit hard. Survival was an instinct we implemented early. We would go to grocery stores and steal food to eat because we didn't have food at home occasionally. Taking food to eat from grocery stores and stealing clothes to wear were a few of the many survival tactics we did together to get by.

We also skipped school because we didn't want to deal with the pressure from bullies. We were out-casted because of the way we dressed and looked. Kids are just mean sometimes, and it made school an agonizing place to be. The bullying would get unbearable for my brother and me. The strain from bullies and not being able to afford the things other kids had taken a toll on us. We had to go without those extras, and we went without - a lot. That was enough stress in itself.

I fought my brother battles when he was afraid to confront them, and I would give him my last when he didn't have. We ran away together, survived foster care together, and supported one another when either of us needed it. He was my other half, and we helped each other get through our rough childhood. In some of our most horrific times, we were there for one another. Our survival depended on sustaining one another. Because of this, we developed an unbreakable bond growing up.

As mentioned before, we were more so best friends. When I made a brainless decision as a child, which most children do, he was right there with me and vice versa. I will forever be my brother's keeper. I love him, dearly. We have had our ups and downs and have forgiven each other countless times after every offense. I am grateful for him being there for me when life hit hard. I couldn't have asked for a better friend to help me get through our childhood most horrific trials and tribulations. I love you to pieces, Big Head, and don't you forget it.

Love Your Family

Friends, boyfriends, fake-friends, and even enemies all came and went, but one thing that always remained was my family. Family is our foundation. It is crucial to maintain a healthy relationship with your family. Family is everything, and we must uphold our family even through the rough times.

Now, if there are toxic family members always hurting you and getting you out of character - draw the line and set boundaries. Distance yourself; therefore, you don't get pulled out of chill mode because of them. Distancing yourself will help with not saying or doing something you'll regret and avoid even more hostility.

With you being the mature and honest one, I know this since your reading this book, pray for them and their growth. Make amends and forgive them for restoring the family bond. Even if restoration isn't possible, that's ok, still, forgive and forget. Pray for their healing, too. Keep your distance to protect your space and heart. Don't harbor it. Just heal and let-go. God is a God of love. He wants us to have happy and sincere relationships, especially with our family and not harboring unforgiveness in our hearts. Love your family until the end.

Chapter 5

Realizing My Brokenness

Now, I was about nineteen years old and room mating with a friend at the time. I was young and starting life out on my own. I worked, went to college, and paid my portion of the few shared bills I was responsible for paying. Life was simple. I didn't have much to worry about at that age in life. Well, at least it sounds that way. There was one big problem; I was emotionally and mentally torn within.

I felt so alone and silently suffered. I carried this for a long time. All the reminiscences from my past rushed back and haunted me. At that point in life, at the age of nineteen, I realized how my history was troubling my present. I'd break down and sob a lot because the things I'd remember about my past was bothering me so much. It was just some things I couldn't let go or get over.

That is when I recognized that I needed healing. My old trauma was very much alive and thriving and negatively affecting me. I felt like the damaged girl within the crew, trying her absolute hardest to be sane. I couldn't genuinely and freely enjoy my young adult life. I had so much going on within me that I was privately battling. I felt like I wasn't connecting with those around me in a way that was, in fact, authentic and natural. I sunk deeper and deeper into the loneliness that soon played a significant role in my depression and insecurities.

Regrettably, I attached to an unhealthy thought that loving a man would make me whole again. I believed that I needed someone else to love me since I didn't know how to love myself. I foolishly assumed my fears and insecurities would somehow go away if this happened – not true! Having this unhealthy thought-process is the single most damaging idea a person could ever have. It's not healthy to put your complete trust in another individual to heal or complete you.

Fix – You – First

It's common for people to think that love can fix them or make them feel complete. This thought is, in fact, far from the truth. If you are not in a peaceful space mentally and emotionally before dating someone, you will, without a doubt, bleed onto them all the hurt and insecurities you never healed from or dealt with, damaging that person in the process.

Furthermore, we all, at some point in life, should have a healthy and loving relationship that uplifts and strengthens us. However, you cannot think that another man or woman can give that to you if you cannot provide that to yourself. That type and magnitude of love only comes from God and is obtained even before you love another person. I don't mean to say that you cannot love someone before or even while your healing – no, not at all. I mean that unless you are both attempting to heal together through God, counseling, or other healing resources while in a healthy space, then only will you both be successful on the journey for that beautiful, honest, and powerful love collectively.

Round and Round We Go

I was on a tireless hunt to get this and hit myself in the head, repeatedly trying to find it, even as early as a teenager. I was searching, guy after guy, and losing a piece of myself every time. Heartbreak after another, I would say the next one would be the one to complete me. I would hurt myself continuously and not even allow myself time to heal from the prior heartbreak. I'd jump from one situation-ship to another. I got so focused on finding a partner instead of focusing on getting myself and mind straight that I didn't even realize that my discernment in character was a huge problem. Whom you chose to attach yourself to tells a lot about yourself. I wasn't secure enough to break free from this harmful pattern of linking to unhealthiness. I would be left wounded and scarred on an even deeper level than before because of false hope and unmet expectations. I wasn't satisfied and at peace with myself. I wouldn't allow God the chance to heal me. I just had to learn and do things on my own idiotically.

I had to be taught the hard way. Even while young, I struggled with horrible thoughts about not being good enough. I gave-in to low self-esteem early in life. I would replay in my head all the awful things I experienced growing up and said to myself I was nothing over and over. That was my routine as a child. That unhealthy thought process broke me down mentally, emotionally, and spiritually.

What I didn't comprehend up until now is that there was a horrible incident I suffered that shaped my harmful frame of mind. The heartbreak I experienced as an innocent child, stole my value and purity early. It was one of many disasters I had to force myself to push through and get over. It broke my virtue, and was the main reason why I stayed looking for real love in all the wrong places – I got raped.

Part 2: Tribulations

I have told you these things so that in Me you may have peace. You will have suffering in this world. Be courageous. I have conquered the world.

~John 16:33

Chapter 6

When Innocence Gets Stolen

Let me take you back to when the rape demon overtook me. I was about seven years old when my innocence got stolen from me. I was gang-raped by three teenage boys who lived in my neighborhood and grew up with me. I was so afraid of them, so I didn't attempt to resist. I wasn't strong enough to fight them off, so I didn't try to struggle or scream. Tears just rolled down my face as I terrifyingly sat there while they forcefully had their way with me. I felt like they were taken out the trash on me, and it was one of the most disgusting feelings I've ever experienced. I was a very young child, and just like that, my innocence and virginity were stolen from me - gone forever.

At the tender age of seven, I endured rape and sexual humiliation in the most disturbing way possible. My mind got so messed up after that. Nothing could ever restore my worth following that rape. I was miserable, good for nothing, and had thought sex to be acceptable. These were my damaging, crucial thoughts as a child. Rape was a silent demon; many young girls experienced. We knew that the offense wouldn't get forcefully addressed since so many young girls go through this and never see justice for the damage done. Due to this heartbreaking reality, many chose to stay quiet, and thus, the rapes continue.

I was hurt and defeated. I kept this trauma hidden deep away from the world. I was confused about myself and sexuality for quite some time after being raped. A lot of young girls and women stay quiet and never tell a soul about being raped. We carry that heaviness for years. We hide it deep within our souls along with the young, innocent girl stolen with it. Your virginity and youthfulness are precious. They can never get replaced after being taken from you.

Molestation

Numerous children suffer rape and molestation. Molestation is when someone, whether it be man or woman, attempts sexual advances or pestering with intentions to have sex with you. Molestation is one deadly evil spirit I knew very well as a child. Growing up, I'd witness many older men deliberately pester underage girls to sit on their lap with hopes they'd be a broken seed that would sooner or later consent to take things further. Those pedophiles ultimately wanted things to end with sex – disgustingly defined as rape! It's never acceptable for an older or young man to make sexual advances on children. Protect our children and address these behaviors immediately; therefore, children will identify what type of action these pedophiles are advancing to right away. Stranger danger!

Rape

Rape is any illicit sexual act done by force with someone underage or incapacitated and, therefore, cannot consent to sex. An incapacitated scenario is when someone has had too many drinks and can't function or have been drugged. Rapist dominates the individual while incapacitated and rapes them. Another form of rape is when a rapist deliberately forces themselves on an adult or disabled person and takes them sexually—defined as a person who can't defend themselves due to being in a wheelchair or blind. A pedophile also attempts to lure a child in, befriend them to gain their trust, and manipulates them into having sex. That's rape. Many children are toyed with because of their gullible innocence and lead to believe the sexual acts they've been subject to perform are inexplicably acceptable.

There have been numerous reports about men raping underage girls for years, and no one knew about it until something drastic happened that forced the secret to reveal. The pedophile had taken advantage of that child and got into their head. Pedophiles make children either believe that rape or molestation is acceptable or that there will be massive repercussions if they tell anyone about it. They manipulate and toy with children's minds in a way they cant comprehend.

Rape Statistics

- Child abuse figures reflect that 39 million Americans were once victims and now survivors of child sexual abuse

- There are over 57,000 reports daily indicating children being victims of sexual abuse in the United States

- Close to 70% of sexually assaulted girl and boy victims are below the age of eighteen

- Out of the 70% of sexual assault victims under the age of eighteen, 82% of the victims are girls

- One out of every nine girls and one out of every fifty-three boys undergo sexual assault

- More than 96% of children raped said they knew their aggressor on a personal level

- The perpetrators have been either family members or close friends initiating the sexual acts

- Out of the findings, 57% were acquaintances, 34% family members, and 7% were strangers.

These statics show a very damaging reality for countless children. To know that so many children are either raped, molested, or both is a frightening epidemic. We have to protect our children. Frankly put, children are our future, and we need to ensure they are safe and feel secure during their childhood.

Rape and molestation are very hard to bounce back from, and even though it can be a hard reality to face, it should never get turned a blind eye. If you know of someone, whether it be a child, man, or woman exposed to rape or molestation, encourage them to get healing and out of that situation in the fastest and safest way possible.

I waited a very long time before I ever mentioned my ordeal with the rape demon, and it was a bad idea to go through life so long without healing in that area. It took a toll on me. I pray that you don't continue to make the same mistake. Be strong. Be encouraged and heal. Don't let the pain from that dark reality take you under and rob you from your joy today. God has a beautiful plan for your life. It's not over for you. Stand firm and take your life back.

Some people chose never to heal because their burdens and pains are too hard to face and handle. I'm asking that you don't accept that route and elevate. Allow God to lift that weight and burden off of you and be set free. Your life is very precious, and you can rewrite the narrative for it. No rape, no pain, nor any other mountain standing in your way blocking your from wholesome has to be the story for you any longer. Heal!

Chapter 7
Stop the Cycle

It's too familiar nowadays for children to get bullied, raped, and sexually humiliated without there being a real curative method put in place for them afterword. Children are out here getting bullied and raped by older kids, strangers, and sadly, by their own family. It is kept undisclosed, hardly addressed, and rarely any therapy provided to children following these traumatic experiences. It is so sad that our babies are undergoing things like this. Many children have to live life as if these experiences never happened. Then, we grow up and don't understand why we cling tightly to toxic and unhealthy behaviors following that trauma. It's all due to broken childhoods and the many unforgettable experiences we endured and never got healing. It is time to stop the cycle

These types of traumatic experiences may have been something you went through, or you may know of someone close to you that went through it as well. The pandemic of sexual abuse has habitually been kept secret and narrowly addressed for too long. The rape demon is a terrifying and dark force; several children get unfortunately subjected to sadly. Lots of us could not get the help necessary to recover from it. We try to live as nothing has ever happened without anyone having the slightest idea what we've endured. We pray without ceasing that our children and their children never have to face such tragedy – ever.

Rape needs to get handled truthfully and head-on. It is crucial to set our children and future generations free. If it is chosen not to address the evil incident of rape head-on, many innocent children will grow into broken adults, and their full healing won't ever take place. Due to this, those unhealthy and toxic behaviors that developed to mask the pain will continue. Following, the idea of getting real spiritual, emotional, or mental therapy to recovery won't be relevant anymore. If this is the case, sadly, many adults assume their pain is manageable, and thus, the unhealthy cycles and toxic behaviors continue.

Protect Our Children

Decide to protect our children. It takes a village to do so. Raising children in a healthy environment is vital. The decisions made concerning a child's mental and emotional health for the long term must come first. If you know that a particular school, neighborhood, or family member threatens the safety and security of your child, leave them and whatever it is alone and don't look back. Keep this conviction and principal in every area of your child's life and ensure that they live by it themselves as they mature.

Consider the long term effects of any decision you chose concerning children. Contemplate and use your best judgment. We want our children psychologically and expressively healthy for them to blossom and grow into mentally and emotionally well adults. It'll be hard to accomplish this if they become victims of uncontrollable trauma, creating stress and anxiety for them that they shouldn't have to handle.

Be Set Free & Let Go

If you were a rape victim, you don't have to live with the toxic psychological aftermath of that dark and evil force any longer. You can become an overcomer. I suffered from the awful turmoil induced by sexual abuse and decided it was time I heal from it. You, also, can lay that burden to rest. It's time to let it all go. The chains have to get broken so that you can live your life to the fullest. When you decide to let it all go, you'll feel that heavyweight from that pain lifts right off of you. You'll begin to make better decisions for yourself, moving forward and let go of unhealthy habits. That will be the most beautiful and satisfying feeling you'll ever experience once you conquer it. You no longer have to force yourself to live with that hurt ever again. We can let it all go together.

I encourage you to do this sooner than later, or you will continue to relive a perpetual cycle of feeling inadequate and dissatisfied with yourself. You'll continue to stay in dysfunctional and unhealthy relationships and stay clinging to new harmful and toxic behaviors that you should be eliminating. The moment you chose to let go and let God is the moment when you'll begin to feel lighter. God will and can free you from any deep-rooted burdens you're refusing to deal with or making the distressing option to bury away to forget.

Diamond In The Rough

For years, I blamed everyone and stayed furious about my virginity getting taken from me in the way that it did. I hated those boys, myself, and everyone around me. I needed someone to hold responsible so that I could continue to fuel my anger and deep-rooted pain.

As I got older and dated, I said to myself that my past was to blame for how things were going in my present. I kept on saying that my relationships were failing because of the baggage from my history. Whew, you talking about being bitter – yes, this was me. However, God's hand was on my life. I had to allow Him to smooth over this rough diamond and break me free from that hateful and shameful mindset I created inside of myself.

It was a hard journey. I cried a lot and silently suffered. I never understood the reason for my behaviors until I fully allowed God into my life and heart. See, as I grew up, I wasn't thinking about God. I didn't understand I fully needed him. My great grandmother was a faithful woman of God and made sure to instill in our family those same values. However, I wanted to do me and didn't have a care in the world about mending my broken heart and trusting God like my mother and great grandmother.

God knew I was running from my pain, and the depths of me were troubled. It was during a very desperate moment where I needed God the most when I realized that the little girl within me was crying and screaming for help. My childhood suffering burdened me. It afflicted me so bad to the point that I didn't even detect the real reason why I continued to act out and rejected the world the way that I did. I was a rebel without a cause and bottled up so much bitterness on the inside. I was angry and felt I had every right to be.

Chapter 8
Foster Care

Foster care is a long-term or temporary residence for children whose parents are unable to care for them due to abandonment, maltreatment, or abuse. This judgment is generally arranged by the state's Child Welfare Agency, formally known as Child Protective Services (CPS). When someone reports maltreatment of a child complaint, an investigation takes place. When grave abuse gets found in the assessment, children are taken into custody and placed with a foster parent. CPS is what we describe in our community as the system. Let me just say that being in CPS custody is not the best place to be.

Foster parents take the responsibility of caring for children while their families rebuild their lives. On occasions, a relative can step in and foster children as well to avoid children from being taken into a foster home, also known as kinship foster care. Children are taken into custody and released when their parents are re-established and able to provide for them a healthier and safer living environment.

Many times social workers are forced to pull children right from their parent's arms at the moment it's decided to take the children into custody. They then place the children into foster care for either short or long term fostering. A short term foster care scenario is when a parent cannot suitably and monetarily provide for their children and thus, has to make the tough decision to comply with the state. Parents have to unveil their uneasy and harsh truth to CPS and succumb to the reality that foster care is not only needed, but required by the state. Parents must comply with the courts' orders before regaining back custody of their children.

During the foster care case, there's court date after court date, along with short, supervised visits with the children, parents, and social worker assigned to the case. The case can take, however long, depending on the amount of time needed before parents are back on their feet, re-established, and other court orders met. A long list of responsibilities and requirements gets fulfilled before the judge rule in the parent's favor. Once requirements are accomplished, children are released from foster care and placed back into their parent's custody.

Foster Care & Me

I went to foster care a total of three times as a child. The first two times, I lived with a state appointment foster parent, and the final time, my auntie decided to step-in as a kinship foster parent for my brother and me. Another stretch in life (not foster care), I lived with two other aunts while a teenager. One was before graduating high school in New York. It wasn't a foster care scenario, but she did save me from possibly having to go back into the system if she had not decided to take me in. After graduating from high school, for a little while, I stayed with another aunt when we all decided to move back to Michigan.

I can never thank my aunts enough for their dedication in making sure I was taken care of during a time I needed them most. It was a tough decision to make to take care of me; however, they made it and stood behind it and didn't look back. I enjoyed growing up knowing that all of my aunts who contributed to caring for me wanted nothing but the best. I'm glad God placed it on their hearts to lend a hand in fostering me until things got back copasetic. Thank you all so much for the time you spent caring for me and the resources you gave for me to lead a happy life. I love ya'll dearly and am forever grateful for the things you all did for us when we needed it the most.

Foster Care Statistics

- In 2017, there were close to 78 million children under eighteen reported in foster care in the United States, accounting for 23% of the population

- The average ages for children in foster care are between the ages of seven and eight

- In foster care, demographics reflect 52% are boys and 48%, young girls

- Surprisingly, 32% of children reported in foster care are living with a relative (kinship foster care), and 45% are with a non-relative foster parent

- Nearly 15% of children undergo horrific violence in their first year within foster-care

- One-third of children placed in foster care described physical, sexual, and emotional abuse happening to them during their time in foster care

- Children describe experiencing severe maltreatment, neglect, and abuse carried out by their caretakers or other children within their foster home

The System

As you can see, there are many cases of abuse reported by children while in foster care, but the controlling agencies have done their best to cover-up and discredit these stories. Covering up children's stories told about their mistreatment in non- relative foster care is done to make the Child Welfare Agency look better-quality than what it is. I mean, how horrible would it be to take children from their families to learn later that they underwent severe abuse during their time in foster care by an individual they never met? As I mentioned before, the system is not a place to be, especially as a child. Children cannot fight or defend themselves and, consequently, become victims of situations they didn't create or can control.

Now, let me say that there is some fit non-relative fostering families out there; however, to know that even one foster family has the potential to damage a child is frightening. Even more alarming to know is that there is mistreatment taking place to children while under the care of the Child Welfare Agency, and parents cannot do anything about it. Parents pray and hope for the best that their children are safe and secure in the home of a stranger while trying to sleep at night. Are you kidding me? You can only imagine how stressful this can be for both the parent and child. The fact that children can be taken from their families and placed in an unfamiliar and perhaps dangerous environment is mind-boggling to me. Just let all that sink in.

Chapter 9

The Truth

Idon't support non-relative foster care and the supporting agencies since I believe they treat children like nothing more than just another number and income source from the state. Let's talk about it. Non-relative foster care is the more common type of fostering, and I by no means liked my foster care experience, even in the slightest. I will dig into my experience a little later; however, this is why CPS is called the "The system." The Child Welfare system isn't always so lovely. Being in foster care is hard enough reality to deal with and wrap your head around as a child. To add to the hard actuality of foster care, it's perplexing to know that many of the caretakers and government agencies do not genuinely care for the welfare of the child.

Not to say that every foster care experience is a bad one; I don't want this to be the idea. I believe foster care primarily was created to support and nurture delicate children by providing them a secure shelter and a healthy living environment during a rough time until their family gets re-established. I do not want to discredit this. Safe and structured foster care is, in fact, a good thing only if this was the truth concerning foster care presently for all the households.

Nonetheless, to truthfully speak, the Child Welfare system has become broken and crooked. If truth be told, reformation is needed. These homes the state is putting children in are not always safe and suitable for fostering a young and delicate soul.

Foster Care through My Eyes

I cannot compare my foster care experience to the next person. I can only speak from my occurrence. However, there are several reports of children and young teenagers who have had bad experiences like the one which I am going to unveil. Getting taken into foster care and going through the whole shebang is a very rough journey. For a child to be placed in the system and undergo even more trauma during their time in foster care is detrimental. Scars from that type of reality don't heal quickly. The reports made by children of molestation, abuse, and grievance of being bounced from house to house prohibiting stability throughout their time within foster care are disturbing.

How are these attributes affecting the welfare of children? Can a child that's already broken be nurtured into wholesomeness undergoing trauma like this while in the system? I highly doubt it. I know this for a fact since I am that child. I lived this life, and I know that life doesn't get any easier mentally and emotionally for kids after going through this type of drama.

Understand that foster care consists of groups of broken children placed all together most of the time with a single parent who may or may not already have biological children living inside the home. Not to mention, they add children of all ages together in a foster home that come from totally different backgrounds and experiences. Often, the other foster children living within the house may have experienced an even harder life than you before being placed into the foster home.

You cannot expect to place a delicate child in an unknown, possibly already broken environment and expect them to recover and not be traumatized following. There are not enough training courses or requisites in the world a foster parent can take to prepare them for dealing with, emotionally providing for, and handling delicate children. The majority of the foster parents are unable to facilitate peace and security for all the children collectively in the home. I know because I've been bounced around to a few foster homes and rarely witnessed a foster parent capable of this myself. Brokenness isn't easy to nurture.

The mental and emotional needs of the children are not met and taken seriously. Children are forced to live with a stranger. Thus, there are extreme isolation and disconnection occurrences because of this. There isn't any real counseling or therapy while in foster care to handle this. Also, due to the bad experiences, children under-go while in foster care, and the extreme isolation, children start to shut down even more. They get pulled from one broken environment and forced to exist in another one. Kids just cannot cope with the harsh reality that comes along with foster care overall.

Chapter 10

My Foster Home

Bedtime was at 8:30 pm sharp every night in my foster home. Night after night, I'd walk up those long narrow stairs to my bedroom that I shared with another foster girl within the household who was older than me. We both had two separate twin-sized beds in our nicely decorated shared room. Our bedspreads were white and yellow with flowers and suns on them. Our room was spacious and delightfully decorated for us. It was a lovely home. This foster parent, in particular, I had lived with at the time, had exquisite taste and decked out her house well. She made sure we kept it cleaned and did chores daily to keep it that way too. I will never forget that.

I had never met this woman before in my life, and now I'm here eating her food and, in return, cleaning her house, and it was the weirdest thing to me. Every day after school, we'd do chores. We'd mop floors, polish the toilets, clean the kitchen, press our school clothes for the week, and had a long list of other chores we were responsible for regularly doing. Each week, the other foster girl and

I would swap duties. The tasks were a little much, but It was her house, so her rules. I just had to do it. I had no other choice. Who was I to change things as the troubled; foster child to challenge that? I just had to roll with it and do as told.

As a child, I didn't understand why I had to get placed in foster care. Before going, I never knew it existed for real. What I did know is that I wanted to leave, and I thought about leaving that lady house every day. I just wanted to go home to my family. I often cried while living there. The other foster girl was mean, unruly, and outright wicked. She bullied me and treated me like crap, and I couldn't do anything about it.

One time, I cried so long and so loud while at the babysitters. I kept yelling, "take me home; I want to go; I want my momma." It was shocking and dramatic the way I sat in that bathroom weeping as all the other kids stared and were confused about why I was sobbing so endlessly the way I was. They didn't know I was in foster care and missed my parents. At that moment, I was about ready to collect my things and run far away from all of them. The sitter had to call my foster parent from work to come and get me since I refused to stop weeping. When she got there, she set me straight. She told me to quit out all that crying and clean my face. It was so firm and reverential the way she scolded me that from that day on, I never cried again about wanting to go home while living in her house.

We Meet Again

On one depressing night, I settled down in my bed, got comfortable, and felt myself dozing off. After falling asleep, I felt her come into my bed to touch and fondle on me again. When I say her, I mean the other foster girl I had no choice to live with and see every day and every night. I wish she'd stop and leave me alone were the thoughts screaming in my head. Anytime she felt like it, she took advantage of me. Forcing her body on mine and having her way whenever she pleased ripping even more of my purity from my fragile soul.

She was older, bigger, and way more violent and manipulative than any other kid I had ever met. I was afraid to stand up to her. I had come faced to face with those same emotions, yet again that I experienced before when those teenage boys in my neighborhood gang-raped me. Motionless and afraid to fight back and even more afraid to repeat the sexual exploitation I underwent while in foster care to anyone. We meet again. I got raped and molested for another time, and it was carried out by a girl in my foster home this time.

I was about nine years old and suffered sexual abuse in the worst ways. I endured a gang-rape by young teenage boys and, after that, got sexually abused by another kid living with me in my foster home. No matter where I went, I did not feel safe or protected. I was a victim at this point. My tears were not seen, nor were my cries ever heard. I was very hopeless. This other rape episode that I underwent again remained a secret and heaviness within me for years too.

As the years went by, I grew increasingly distant and was misconstrued by those around me because of it. I felt like I had no one who truly understood what I was going through on the inside. I didn't feel secure in my own body. Rape and molestation were prevalent in my standard of living, and I felt like nothing positive would come from me, revealing my torment to anyone. Would they even believe me? Does anyone even care? It seems like sexual abuse often happens in my life, so let me bottle it up and never deal with it was my conclusion and diagnosis for myself. I struggled to reveal the truth about my sexual abuse for years and decided now is the time to speak out finally. No more guilt. Nor more shame. I will no longer be a victim.

<u>No Longer a Victim</u>

If you've suffered sexual abuse, I want you to know that you no longer have to be a victim. The thoughts you may have about yourself and the rape you endured doesn't have to be a mountain standing before you. God loves you and wants you unbound from all that. He will never leave nor forsake you. God is with you, even during the darkest moments of your life. Those dark moments may have been in your past, or they may be your present. It doesn't matter when or where those darkest moments have taken place in your life; God wants to be that Strong Tower for you whenever needed. That time is now.

When I allowed God to heal me, as stated before, significant burdens got lifted off my shoulders - the weight of low self-esteem, promiscuity, not feeling worthy, self-sabotage, and so many other lies I told myself that was not true. I began to walk with my head held higher and higher. I felt better and relieved as the days went by. Right before my eyes, the changes within me took place. I was no longer afraid to walk in my purpose. The damage from all the things that tore me down from the inside out got reversed and undone. I am a walking testimony. I said to myself, "I will no longer be a victim!"

We live our lives keeping pain buried away without ever addressing it. Doing this doesn't have to be your reality any longer. We need to do the exact opposite – face our fears. Tell our story. Bless another soul with our testimony. It's time to heal, no more burying pain! No longer do you have to conceal the agony from molestation or whatever else you may be dealing with or have undergone. No longer does it have to remain a yoke to your heart, mind, and emotions. Let go. Let God. He got you.

Chapter 11
Physical Abuse

Iendured substantial physical abuse as a child. The cruelty I suffered included being thrown across the room, punched, slapped, stomped on, choked, and any other type of horrific physical abuse you can imagine. All of the physical abuse I endured was accompanied by verbal and emotional neglect, as well. The verbal abuse I experienced involved getting called profane, curse words, and receiving overly harsh chastisement not suitable for a child. Criticism, belittling, abandonment, threats, ridicule, and extreme punishments were examples of some of the emotionally abusive dealings I received as a child.

Abuse is fatal to undergo at any age, above all, as a child. Your perception of family, life, relationships, and love become very jaded and toxic following if you don't heal from it. Any type of abuse children experience can shape them crookedly if they don't get the required counseling or therapy to recover. Being abused in any form can affect how you interact with the world. You're never the same after that type of shock. I'll say that again. "You're never the same." Whether it be physical, emotional, mental, or even spiritual, it's hard to recuperate from any abuse. I continued to spiral out of control because of the abuse I endured. My confidence and sense of security were all stolen from me due to the violence and neglect. I got deprived of my virtuousness and child-like mentality way before time.

<u>A Night I'll Never Forget</u>

I remember one abusive episode, in particular, as if it was yesterday. I thought my brother and I were going to die or get admitted into the hospital after the brutality we suffered this day. It was a regular night for us. My brother and I were eating, and after a few bites of food later, I saw a garbage bag fly across the room at us. It's an extremely filthy feeling to have garbage thrown at you. Piercing curse words got yelled at us, and eerie grunts shouted. Before we could even move, I saw my brother get snatched by the throat. His head was lifted and slammed on the wall repeatedly. His little body was dangling from beneath him. We were beaten and shouted at for reasons unknown to us. It all came out of nowhere. I afterward started to get slapped in the face and punched on the head several times. It was so much force and energy behind those slaps and punches that I have a lifelong scar at the very top of my head because of them. The damage from the injury at the top of my head bled out on my scalp. The blood was soaked up by my thick locks and stained the top of my hair red for two weeks until my hair got done again.

I was afraid of what might have happened to my brother and me if I told anyone about this abuse. I ended up lying about the scar altogether. I kept the scar and our abuse secret. I later learned that I could have died from that type of injury to my head as a small child. Let me remind you, my brother and I were little kids, no older than the age of six and nine when this took place. Because of my judgment to keep our abuse secret, my brother and I underwent more physical abuse subsequently -silently suffering. In the long run, my brother and I made a collective decision that enough was enough. We found refuge and way out of the horrible physical abuse and violence. We never looked back.

Another Episode I'll Never Forget

Another horrific abusive episode I experienced as a child was when I got snatched by my face then dragged outside with no shoes on my feet. It was during the wee hours of the night, It was cold, and the abusive verbal words yelled at me were earsplitting. I was afraid, and it woke up the entire block.

Later on, I got smacked in the face some more, slammed on the floor, and stumped on. My little body was so bruised up and scarred. For a long time, I had a long scratch on the left side of my cheek from being snatch by my face and nails dug in my skin. It took years for that scar to heal and was a constant reminder of another episode of physical abuse I'd never forget.

Abuse Statistics

- Physical abuse is the number one form of abuse children experience in the United States

- Sexual abuse second, emotional neglect and abuse third, and physical neglect following

- In 2014, almost 1,600 children died from neglect and abuse

- That's roughly four to five children that die from abuse and neglect daily

- There're 6.6 million children involved in cases reported to The Child Protective Services yearly concerning child abuse or neglect cases

- One study found that 80% of young adults had at least one psychological disorder due to childhood abuse

- Severe abuse in children has long term effects that follow them well into adulthood

- Some effects include mental health disorders, addictions, sexual, and reproductive issues

- When abused children become adults, they are more likely to become victims of domestic violence, adopt alcoholism, become substance abusers, undergo depression, and are suicidal

- An alarming 14% of women and 36% of men incarcerated suffered abuse as a child

The Aftermath

The abuse I suffered, wretchedly, got engraved in my mind, heart, and spirit. That abuse produced a rage within me that would come out in a hot second if I got pushed to the limit. I took my anger and frustrations out from the abuse on school peers, and sadly, on my little brother too. I was supposed to protect him, in opposition; I failed because I was a wrecked child from all the cruelty and negligence I bore. I began to embody the hurt and abuse. I couldn't have power over myself - over the aftermath. It was a malevolent cycle that needed to end.

The abuse caused me to become violent, disorderly, and I desperately needed to get counseling or some type of therapy;   insolence, fighting, arrogance, lying, a sneak, and promiscuity were all toxic habits I urbanized due to my trauma. My performance in school was below average, and my attitude and demeanor grew more and more distorted, leading into my teenage years. I got put out of the house in the end at the age of sixteen. Termination of our parent-child relationship was created. I was given-up rights to go live my aunt in New York state. I wasn't allowed to live with my mother or father at the time.

I didn't know how to articulate my built-up frustrations and pain. The appropriate counseling and therapeutic remedies I so very much needed after those abusive episodes as a child were not available to me. And thus, I grew into a very problematic adolescent. I became a trouble maker for my parents, brother, and teachers. Looking back, I regretted everything, and I ultimately wished my life would have been different.

I continued down a vicious cycle of defiance and became a product of my environment for many years before I was set free. I was searching and trying so hard to fill that void. I was depressed and didn't believe I deserved better. I thought this to be my reality. I did so many bad things in life that half of the stuff I did, I don't even want to repeat. I didn't know anything other than brokenness and drama. It took some time for me to begin to see things clearly, but eventually, I got there. It took me taking a stance and wanting better for myself and getting fed up with the false reality of myself I fashioned in my mind

Chapter 12

Psychiatric Hospital

For a short period in my childhood, I was admitted into a mental and behavioral hospital because I would experience black-outs periodically. It was a terrifying incident for me. During my black-outs, no one could seem to wake me up or snap me back to sense. I would get unresponsive, or I'd aimlessly stare into space – motionless and withdrawn.

These black-out spells would happen to me at school or home at any given time. No one knew the triggers that caused them. It became a mind-boggling experience for the doctor and my mother on trying to figure out my problem. The doctors concluded and suggested I get admitted to a psychiatric hospital for children who have unexplainable behaviors and may be experiencing mental and emotional distress.

I didn't want to go and leave my family. I was still in elementary school when this all took place. I was beyond burdened at this point in life. Against my will, I was shipped off, away from my family, and admitted into a hospital with other children that were experiencing disturbances worst than mines. You can only imagine how hard it was for me to process all this as a child. I was hurt and heartbroken all over again. I had to carry yet another yoke. I had to push myself through some more pain with hopes of things being better for me on the other side – yet again.

Alone

Going to the psychiatric hospital did something severe within me. I found myself alienating mentally and zoning out regularly. I wanted to push those around me out. However, the doctors were trying their hardest to do the opposite and find their way within. I cried, cried, and cried while there. I wasn't at ease at all. I couldn't stand being away from my family in the most unfamiliar place in the world to me. Was I a mental patient? Did I reach my breaking point, and did it cause me to have black-outs? I haven't even finished elementary school, why would they suggest this? Whom can I trust here? Why do I have to take so many pills, and why are the doctors calling me a risk?

Even though it was a short period in my life, I didn't enjoy the hospital staff, the food, or medicine. I didn't believe that I needed to be there. As a child, I just didn't understand why. Why was all this happening to me? I asked myself this every day. I was so young and had no clue as to why my life was unraveling the way it was. I didn't want to wake-up in my shoes day after day because my life was just a mess. I wanted to trade places with another child. A child that wasn't so heavily burdened and didn't have to overcome the obstacles I had to oblige myself to beat. I wanted to switch lives with a child dealt a better hand than I was in life. I wanted my life to get reshuffled. My life could not be real.

Looking back, that period in my life, residing in that hospital, left a grave disfigurement within my soul and heart. I saw things in other children that I had never seen before. I felt the behaviors, and the tone of the hospital was that of an apocalypse. We were all there due to being mentally and emotionally unsound, and that was a harsh reality to face. I tried to forget those all-white walls, those all white sheets, and swallowing all those pills three times daily. Going through those black-out spells was already a lot to deal with, and having to wake-up every day in a mental hospital was a whole other mountain in itself. It was a lot to handle, and I was in that hospital left to feel it all on my lonesome.

Statistics

- Psychiatric disorders change the way children typically learn, behave, or manage their emotions which creates problems for them daily

- The more frequent disorders in children in the U.S. are ADHD, behavior problems, anxiety, and depression

- 4.5 million children, between 3-17, are diagnosed with anxiety and 1.9 million with depression

- Anxiety diagnosis has increased in children from 5.5% in 2007 to 6.4% in 2011–2012

- Amongst children between 2–8, every 1 and 6 (17.4%) has a diagnosis of a mental, behavioral, or developmental issue in the United States

- Children aged 6–11 are more likely to have behavior problems than children in any other age group

- Boys between 2-8 were more likely than girls to have a mental, behavioral, or developmental disorder

- Age and poverty level is a determining factor in the accessibility of children receiving treatment for anxiety, depression, or behavior problems

Mental health is vital. I did not fully understand that my black-outs correlated to the rough life I lived, which was the root of all my problems. I was a repressed child and had a bunch of suppressed emotions. What I was dealing with on the inside was far more significant than what my little mind and body could handle. The harsh truth of this induced my black-outs.

I was far too young to comprehend the treatment I received or grasp anything beneficial out of my time away in the hospital. What I do know is that it broke my soul to have to go through it during the time I did. It was something that took time to get over, and it didn't happen right away. Once released, I never told anyone about my time away in that hospital. My lips stayed sealed. I was too ashamed to repeat it before. I boldly decided to share and express my feelings for the first time and stand firm in my truth; so, I can move on from it and encourage anyone else who has battled this war before. You are not alone.

Chapter 13

An Ill Legacy

After reading the first two parts of this book, you can see that I needed to heal from a lot. A lot happened to me that I had no control over growing up. That is an even more disturbing fact about my childhood. The fact that I could not change my circumstances; the fact that I could not escape; and the fact that the way I lived and knew life was a jaded realism.

I knew no better. All I knew was what stood before me – shattering and tragic circumstances. I didn't know that I required healing. No one ever discussed this to me. I didn't learn about healing in foster care or even in the hospital. The hospital only wanted to dope us up and leave us isolated for hours at a time. My actuality consisted of a sad and ill legacy of pain and burden children forced to grow up in dysfunctional cycles. That's not fair or right for innocent children to grow up this way.

To be secure both mentally and emotionally in this world as an adult, you first need a civilized and healthy upbringing as a child. It starts at home. Enlightened instruction must take place way before teenagers walk across the stage at high school for their graduation; way before their road test for a driving permit; way before middle school; before elementary; before their little legs are strong enough to walk; in the womb. Emotional, mental, and spiritual security and stability starts at home. Parents are the teachers of this at all times.

We need to ensure that our children are safe. I've said this before. Our children need to learn, witness, and be taught security by the actions we take and choose daily as parents. Innocent children should not be left burdened with pain due to circumstances out of their control. We have to keep them safe. Safe also means making sure they do not get abused mentally, emotionally, or physically. Even if you lived a burdened life as a child, you could change that reality for your children. The ill legacy doesn't have to continue. You don't have to pass burdens down. Things can change and be different, and the choice is yours. I am a firm believer in this. The bondage and yoke can get broken. Stop the ill legacy and break free from that abusive and horrifying oppression and generational curses.

Rebuild

Create a new legacy for your bloodline. Heal from the oppression and create a wholesome and healthy legacy for the generations to come. Set your mind up that from this day forward, you will rebuild. Rebuild your mind. Rebuild your heart. Rebuild your way of thinking. Rebuild your life. Rebuild your children's lives. Rebuild your finances. Rebuild your relationships. Rebuild your friendship. Rebuild your future. Rebuild! Rebuild! Rebuild!

You and your family will not get taken under because of the horrible events from your past. Even if things are going on presently that's bringing you down or threatening you or your child's security, you can be set free from it. You don't have to stay in any situation that is inhibiting you from being healed and whole. Let it all go and move on. The choice is yours. Today is an excellent day to rebuild your present and the future. The past can never be changed and will forever be a part of you. But, it doesn't have to define you. You are not and will no longer be a product of your past.

There's nothing wrong with starting over. With the help of God and useful resources, and an environment conducive to healing, things can be better for you. Do not stay in a cycle of an ill legacy. Be set-free. Over the next few chapters, I'll explain some healing remedies and resources that helped me and is still helping me to this day, along with the help of God. They have also helped others just like you to triumph over life's most challenging moments.

No, I am not perfect, and yes, I still do make mistakes. However, I can say that my determination to break free from ill legacies and bondage, has kept me moving in the right direction ahead. I am no longer a statistic or a product of my old environment and old self. I vowed that my children won't ever witness or experience the turmoil I saw and bore. My bloodline will be victorious! Declare this for you and your family. You got this.

Part 3: Manifest Healing

"Daughter," He said to her, "your faith has made you well. Go in peace and be free from your affliction."

~Mark 5:34

Chapter 14
Healing

The word healing is "the change to becoming healthy again or regaining a sound mind." The word regaining means taking something back into your possession. When you heal, you choose to reclaim the reality of the state of mind you once had before your pain. This explanation means that when we decide to repair, our mind snaps back to a pre-painful state. We conclude that our pain won't hurt or burden us anymore. When we get restored, there's no perversion, no confusion, or callousness that takes place in our train of thoughts in the effect that it did during our painful state. We beget security and clearness. Ultimately, when we heal and regain wholesomeness, it's because we conquered it within our minds first.

Healing is necessary for all living things on this earth: including animals, plants, and every other creature breathing and existing on this planet. We all experience pain at some point in our life, and thus, require healing following. When we experience something painful, we have a choice. We can allow it to change us for good or for the worst. I so earnestly wish everyone choose the road to healing not only for yourself but because God wants it for you.

When we heal, we grow. Healing is significant for our mental, emotional, and physical development. We function at our best when we are whole, repaired, and set-free from our afflictions. When healed, we think uprightly. We operate with a sound mind, are less stressed concerning the cares of this world, and can I mention, we become more of ease to be around. Some folk can get to a real sour state and are hard to be around when they are troubled and clouded with pain. Due to this, they project their pain on everyone else and utterly oblivious of their coldhearted actions. Don't be this way; chose to be set free. When healed, our presence is lighter, brighter, and we are more level headed naturally. Logically, we can provide the best part of ourselves to those around us and not get weighed down with things we once let keep us bitter and uneasy when we are set on the path to being set free.

<u>While Injured</u>

When a person is injured physically, they become immovable. They can't move or function as quickly as someone who is physically able. People who are injured move slower and those around them have to help and sustain them since they can't function on their own due to their injury. Being injured physically is the same as being wounded mentally and emotionally.

The aftermath of your pain can either strengthen and develop you or disable you and leave you stuck in a toxic mindset. If you chose to stay trapped in a toxic mindset, unhealthy patterns start and grow worse over time. Don't allow it. Enable yourself to grow and vibrate higher.

<u>Are You Refusing to Heal?</u>

Think about it, are there trials in your life you face often? What's going on inside blocking your blessings? Are there any hard feelings you're dealing with now? Is there any ill emotion, stigma, or schemes running through your blood that you're refusing to let go? Are you replaying a heartbreaking episode that happened to you in your mind causing you to stay trapped in bitterness, hurt, and unforgiveness? Have you decided not to let your guard down and let go? Are you refusing to heal form something?

It's hard to look within and confess some truths. That takes courage and pure honesty. I can admit to this because I had to do the same thing. As mentioned in my opening, I had to face my fears, take accountability, and get real with myself. Most importantly, I had to come to terms with some things that I had chosen not to speak of or face ever again. There were so many distressing things that happened to me that the bad things I experienced haunted me and created nightmares. I never received an apology. I never got an 'I'm sorry." Due to this, I stubbornly said I wouldn't let go or forgive. Nevertheless, it needed to be done. I had to press on and continue to reach my highest potential regardless of an explanation or apology.

See, you never know pain until you have to face life without a healing almanac and are forced to play like nothing ever happened to you for real. Or, when you are considered the problem in a world where you had no choice but to grow up in straight dysfunction and toxic-ness. In a world where you never hear, "I apologize, or I was wrong for what I did and caused you to be." A life like this is taxing. The grudges I kept where becoming heavy. I had to allow myself to blossom. I had to deal with my wrong actions and shortcomings ultimately. I couldn't give out anymore hate and exert miserable energy in the world any longer. God would vindicate me in the long run.

Some things we are not healing from or getting over are often things we are afraid to face. It's too emotional. Being transparent with yourself requires genuine openness and vulnerability that we persistently refuse to confront. Refusal to do this will cause you to get tested regularly. Your pride, mindset, and judgment will all be the target for the test because of obstinancy. Perpetual tough obstacles will come about frequently in your life when you reject growth. When you don't rise above your pain and face the truth, voids develop.

Voids

I used to hit myself in the head hard. I'd search for all types of voids in all the wrong places. This ultimate void I was searching for was a pure love I needed to give myself. I was seeking to fill that void within, and I'd try to fill it with all types of toxic and unhealthy things. I'd get caught up with the wrong crowds and disconnect myself further and further from God's truth about me and how He indeed saw me. I'd do things so awful and belittle myself so much that I would proclaim myself undeserving and inadequate to deserve better.

My self-worth was damaged. I took the approval of others with more importance than God's approval. I felt I was nothing and deserved the very little I was settling for. I had no healthy outlet to aide me with reaffirming my worth as a young child, as a teenager, or as a young woman. With undergoing rape, molestation, and many other unspeakable adversaries, life had a tight grip on me, and I believed that I was nothing more than what the societal statistics said I was going to be.

Holding this yoke caused me to grasp even tighter to destructive behaviors. I created a counterfeit and unwholesome image in my mind about what I deserved because I suffered so much in life. I thought I deserved the pain that came from my past and bad life choices. I foolishly believed it was acceptable to settle for very little because I was a torn soul. I clung tight to the thought that the unhealthy cycle I chose to live in and created was necessary to fill my void and emptiness. Having these types of ideas was perilous to my emotional and mental health. I fell into a spiral of bad decisions and toxic behaviors because I didn't love myself enough.

I degraded myself over and over again because I wouldn't choose the path of healing. My dark past got the best of me. I got told I should've got aborted, that I was nothing but practice for men until they find their wives, and that I wasn't gone amount to anything because I was ruthless and wild, sorrowfully, I believed and accepted that deception in my mind. There are life and death in the tongue. I took any, and every evil thing said about me and held it tight. It produced in my heart a torn soul that needed significant restoration and redemption.

As time progressed, I continued to fall deeper and deeper into my unhealthy patterns, losing a piece of my heart and mind every time. Bad relationships, fake friendships, and plenty of other lousy life choices following. I refused intervene to allow God to since I was embarrassed, ashamed of myself, and fearful. I thought that I didn't deserve restoration.

Stand Tall

One day, I just got up and said to myself, "not anymore." I stood tall and held my head high. I got tired of the mess. I took a stance against drama and decided not to be embarrassed, ashamed, or guilty anymore. I got determined to triumph over all of my life's messiest and heartbreaking moments. I chose to heal and to stand in my truth. I am bigger and higher than every unhealthy, lousy habit I once clung tight to and told myself I needed and couldn't let-go.

Healing isn't an overnight process, for real. It requires real revelation and submission to the truth. Submitting to integrity takes a while, depending on how ready and willing you are concerning facing your fears and letting go of the dead weight you carried over the years. Look within and be as transparent as possible with yourself on a profound level. Be honest and face your truth. What are you burying away and refusing to face?

I know that many of you reading this book may have undergone a lot worse than I have. I know that you're sad, perplexed, silently battling, and misunderstood. This was me. Cry, let it out, and submit to the truth that it is time to heal and let it all go. Allow God to come in to be that helping hand and Cornerstone for you. You're not alone. Don't carry that weight any longer by yourself.

You Got This

Accept this reality: Healing is manifesting in your life. You are needed, attractive, intelligent, above, and not below. The lies you told yourself are not true about being valueless and undeserving. You're not alone. God loves you, and it's time you start believing it. Manifest healing now, you got this!

Chapter 15

Manifestation

Manifestation is "the action or reality showing an intangible idea." Other words used to describe intangible are impossible, difficult, invisible, or spiritual. In other words, things can come into existence all due to your thoughts and beliefs. When something manifests itself in your life, it's because you have called it forth. You have continually given energy towards something so strongly in your mind and thoughts that it became real. Be careful with your words and thoughts. Whatever you conceive in your mind and heart will materialize and come into existence, manifesting itself.

To manifest healing, you have to earnestly believe that you're healed regardless of your current natural state. You have got to call it forth. The word manifest is also considered a verb, so you must take action. Take action towards your healing. When you manifest something, you are in process mode.

Strictly speaking, you have to believe in your mind that it doesn't matter what the medical report says, you will manifest healing despite the diagnosis. It doesn't matter what horrible past traumas you went through; you're going to manifest healing despite your past traumatic ordeals. It doesn't matter how emotionally, mentally, or spiritually torn you may feel; you're going to manifest healing regardless of any and everything opposing you. You will snap back to that pre-hurtful frame of mind.

The Wrong State of Mind

On the other hand, manifestation can go either way. In the wrong state of mind, you can manifest the wrong things. Have you noticed that when something terrible happens to you, it messes with you mentally and sometimes physically? You think and dwell on it over and over. During that time, you replay every unfortunate aspect of that incident in your brain, stressing and worrying yourself out about it. Then boom, like a thief in the night, something else unfortunate happens leading into a long trail of other unlucky things happening following. The reason for this is because you have manifested something else unpleasant in your life due to your thoughts.

Whatever is inside of you can manifest itself at any time in your life. That's why it's harmful to hold grudges and dwell on negative feelings all the time. Let them go! I used to cling tightly to very toxic and evil thoughts about myself. I was unforgiving and held grudges often. Due to harboring all this mess in my heart, I manifested a lot of bad things in my life. I wasn't happy with myself. The energy and power I gave those negative thoughts and feelings produced a cycle of depressing things to materialize into existence.

It wasn't until I begin to accept purely positive, uplifting, and healing thoughts when I elevated higher and prospered. You are what you think. If you believe highly and healthily, you'll manifest just that.

Once you let go of unhealthy thinking and toxic behaviors, you'll begin to see life differently. You won't give energy to things that'll bring you down. You won't sweat the small stuff anymore. No more of your time will go towards circumstances that bring you down, and you'll start to focus and attract an enriching and brighter reality. Don't waste any more of your time on thoughts that drain the light out of you. Hold ya' head high and say, "I got this!" Start manifesting and attracting abundance today!

Law of Attraction

The Law of Attraction is a theory that we can produce our reality, and this theory resonates with me so profoundly. According to this law or philosophy, we have the power to attract whatever it is we want, and on the contrary, whatever it is, we don't as well. We invite all things to prosper in our world through our thoughts and emotions.

The Law of Attraction is a rhythmic frame of mind and emotions. It's a metaphysical and spiritual decree from within. When you think and feel something very strongly, the forces and energies of that which you are thinking, feeling, and giving power to, will attract to you. Limited thinking will produce a finite reality. Positive, boundless beliefs; and mindsets will manifest that same reality in your life.

Metaphysical & Biblical

The Bible has a lot to say about our frame of mind and the way we think. There are several scriptures in the Bible relating to the Law of Attraction. The Bible doesn't mention the literal expression of " Law of Attraction;" however, the principles are still the same in various scriptures. I will list a few scriptures below and elaborate more on how God wants us to have a positive and encouraging mindset about all things in life, especially our healing. Once again, we are what we think.

Then He touched their eyes, saying, "Let it be done for you according to your faith!"

~Mather 9:29

God healed two blind men according to their faith. They believed without a shadow of a doubt that they will be cured. Got will indeed meet you at your level. He can only operate at the highest magnitude in your life if you allow Him. The level of faith you have will determine the amount of power God can display in your life. If you have limited faith, it will only yield limited power.

The Kingdom of Heaven is within you

~ Luke 17:21

We have Godly and Heavenly energies within us. God placed it inside us all. We are created in His image and likeness (Genesis 1:27). We have like-minded thoughts and authority just as Jesus does and can draw and manifest good things in our life.

Set your mind on what is above, and not what is on this earth

~Colossians 3:2

Thinking on things spiritual, heavenly, and edifying will keep your heart, mind, and spirit in a positive and liberating place. These are the things we want to gravitate to us in life. These are things we should always meditate over.

As a man thinks in his heart, so is he

~ Proverbs 23:7

Whatever is within the depths of your mind, heart, and soul is your truth and reality. Whether this reality is dark or light, it will attract to you. Why not internalize honest and pure things in your heart; therefore, the same will be invited in your life?

I can do all things through Him who strengthens me
~Philippians 3:14

God wants you to know that anything is possible, and He is with you, even during the weak times. Keep your mind open to this truth, and it will catapult you to achieve amazing things.

Do not be conformed to this age, but be transformed by the renewing of your mind. So that you may discern what is the good, pleasing, and perfect will of God.
~Romans 12:2

Don't think as everyone else thinks. Renew your chain of thoughts regularly, primarily if your thoughts serve no gratifying purpose. God wants us to maintain the right frame of mind; so, we can work alongside Him to materialize good things.

Get Rooted

I encourage you to read more of these scriptures in your alone time to get a fresh perspective from your point of view. Push yourself to break free from your old, casual frame of mind that attempted to leave you restricted. Make a solid decision now to get rooted in God's word. Get rooted in God's truth about your life and not what the world says about you. Get rooted in a new frame of mind that will benefit you now and for the future generations to come. Get rooted in manifesting abundance!

Chapter 16

What Are You Rooted In?

When our mind is rooted in something, whether good or bad, we unconsciously produce that reality in our daily lives. For instance, when wanting to lose weight, we begin to think to eat healthier, exercise more, and make better decisions concerning our health. The goal is to lose weight; therefore, we believe and do things necessary to make weight loss a reality. Thus, weight loss and healthier habits manifest in our lives. It all started with a thought.

On the other hand, if you are pessimistic, feel unworthy, and are fearful, you'll by no means reach your full potential all due to your fickle thinking. Those around you will also perceive this. Fearful, undeserving, and capricious thoughts will keep you stagnant and prohibit you from reaching your full potential. It robs you from everlasting joy. The time wasted on negligent thinking is what I'd like to call it, it's precious time you can never get back.

Change Our Children

Get rooted in good things that'll manifest and attract an abundant life for you and your family. That will add value to your days. Think and speak life to yourself and your surroundings and especially to your children. If you speak life and abundance into your children along with being an admirable example as a parent, they'll manifest and attract healthy and respectful behaviors in their life. On the flip side, if you talk down to your children and repudiate being an ethical and responsible example, they'll exhibit the same habits.

I'm not saying this will be the reality for all children. Some children are resilient and, regardless of their upbringing, still function at their very best. That's a real blessing indeed. However, most children who have had callous parents and a terrible childhood don't bounce back. It's hard to unlearn that damage. A dramatic change must get made for the next generation. The one thing that keeps generational curses alive in families is the refusal to change and the absence of healing resources.

Generational Change

If a family bloodline was once rooted in rape, poverty, drugs, bad health, mediocrity, fearfulness, gang-banging, abuse, rage, obesity, corruption, and many other bad attributes for generation after generation without change, it's all because of unchanged behaviors and thinking. Generational change is vital for our children and their children so they can be afforded a healthy and upright life. Dismissal of change prohibits this. It is up to you to be the one to change things for your children and their children—No-more ill legacies.

Change your lifestyle to promote wealth and good health. Protect children and pay close attention to the things that go on in their lives and the people they hang around. Be present, be available, and be supportive. To cultivate an enjoyable and peaceful legacy for our children, we must first show them the way. Let your child know that life will be different for them, regardless of the past. There is a brighter future. Show the future generations that you can manifest healing and that you can attract abundance to live a happy and healthy life. Doing this will cultivate a generational change.

No More Permission

To achieve generational change, you must first get rid of those bad things that have held you back. These are the things you've condoned and given permission to stay prevailing in your life. Do not provide any more authority to damaging and toxic things any longer to remain dominant in your world. Get rid of the things that distract you from healthy living and generational change. Most importantly, do not look for and create new unhealthy outlets while you're on the pathway to healing and breakthrough.

Toxic and unhealthy behaviors stay prevalent in our life because we chose not to face them or let them go. These toxic habits are prevailing in our life because they got passed down to us, or it was what we witnessed growing up. Generation change kicks in here. Say it with me, "No more permission!" All we need is one family member to stand tall and hold their head high and say no more, and the rest will follow their example. All we need is one family member to decide not to continue in the same way that their parents, grandparents, or great grand-parents did to break the bloodline free from generational curses.

I know you were dealt a bad hand in life. I know it's hard, and you may feel that it cannot get done or was possible before. I am here to share with you that it will get done, and you are the one to do it. You are that family solider and prime example for change. Your children and their children's lives depend on it.

God is looking and waiting for you to make that decision and walk with Him. He knows your pain and wants to show you the way. God doesn't want things to continue on the way they have. He wants affluent and blessed legacies after you. Allow God to work at it with you. Break free from bondage and take that leap of faith. Faith without works is dead. Come on now; God got you.

Chapter 17

Faith

Faith is having complete trust and confidence in something or someone. Another definition provided by the King James Bible dictionary is that "faith is the persuasion of the mind that a certain statement is true." There goes the mind again. It's a proven fact that whatever feeling you experience must pass through your brain first, even the sentiment of faith. When you have faith in something, you believe in it whole-heartedly, yet when things around you show that, you should lose trust and let-go. Your brain gets set up to trust that it doesn't matter what's going on or what it looks like; you will still have faith. You decide to reset and persuade your mind daily to have faith in whatever it is you choose. We can put our faith in anything we want to.

Faith is a hopeful frame of mind. It's that feeling you get when you close your eyes, bow your head, and whisper, "God, I trust you." Faith is kept close to your heart and placed deep within your spirit.

Faith has to be maintained and renewed daily. It's like a good luck charm. You check your faith (good luck charm) daily, and it gets you through the highs and lows. It sustains us through times when we grow weak in spirit. It's light, yet powerful. It starts small then grows over time. Faith remains with us until the full manifestation of our deepest desires becomes a reality.

Faith Building Scriptures

To have faith in God and yourself, you must believe what The Bible says concerning God's view towards us and faith. The Bible has many scriptures on faith. God makes it clear that we need faith to make things a reality and conquer battles in our life. I encourage you to study and read the full scriptures in more depth and other faith-building scriptures on your own time as well to build and renew your faith daily.

For I know the plans I have for you' – this is the Lord's declaration –'plans for your peace and not for evil, to give you a future and hope.

~Jeremiah 29:11

This scripture is my favorite. This scripture lets me know that God plans for you and me are to be prosperous and blessed. Anything besides this isn't the truth. God loves us dearly, and you have to understand He plans for our victory over any and everything.

I have been beautiful and wonderfully made

~Psalms 139:14

God took His time with you. You are precious and perfect in His eyes. Know that you are lovely and treasured in any case.

By His stripes, we are healed

God died on The Cross for us. Because of His suffering, we are restored and set free. You don't need to accept bondage.

We are more than a conqueror
~Romans 8:37

You can do all things and move any mountain that stands before you. You are a defeater and its time that you believe it.

Our sins are forgiven (Isaiah 43:25).

God knows that we all fall short of the glory (Romans 3:23). He knows we mess up, and He gives us room to mature and learn from our mistakes. Forgiveness is available to us all.

In Christ, we are a new creation, and old things have passed away
~2 Corinthians 5:17

When we give our lives to Christ, we are no longer the same. We inherit new things spiritually, physically, and emotionally. Out with old; in with new.

No weapon formed against us will prosper
~Isaiah 54:17

There may be attempts to attack your character, your heart, your credibility, and everything else, but God got you. Do know that they won't defeat you or prosper.

God loves us so much that he laid down his life for us
~Romans 8:5

For those of you who have children know that you would do anything for your child, including dying for them. You love them just that much and want to protect them at all costs. Well, this is how much God loves you too. He loves us so much that he died for us. Now, that's unconditional love.

These are just a few faith-building scriptures that are in the Bible, but there's plenty more. Place your favorites in plain sight to be recited and viewed daily to build and grow your faith. Whatever area in life you're weak in, God has an authoritative scripture to strengthen it just for you. BIBLE = Basic Instructions For Life. God has beautiful and peaceful plans for you. You won't reach your fullest potential if you stay in a pessimist frame of mind. Meditate on excellent and pleasant ideas concerning your life; so, you can build your faith and attract the same to you.

Chapter 18
Start Small

Keep faith alive, no matter what. When we read God's word continually, it cultivates space in our heart for faith to strengthen and develop. Starting with a small seed of faith will grow into immovable faith in time. As mentioned before, we have to persuade our minds that healing is true regardless of the circumstances. Once you trust and believe without a shadow of a doubt that you are what God says you are and forget about what others think, you'll see how smoothly your life and mindset will change.

The more knowledge you get in God's word, the more your faith will increase. Its proven truth that the more knowledge you gain on a topic, the more your faith will grow in it. Knowledge builds faith. It's just like studying for a school subject or learning a new language. You'll trust yourself more and more to execute effortlessly following gaining more knowledge in that topic and studying. This fact serves the same concerning studying and learning God's Word – He's the topic!

Your faith will get so fixed on good things after learning what God says about His love towards you that nothing else will matter. Everything else will soon fade away that doesn't coincide with your faith. You'll love and forgive effortlessly and get so much joy out of life. It's the best feeling in this world as His truth about His Love unfolds right before your eyes and heart.

What Do You Have Faith In?

Did you know that people can put their faith in many things, even if it serves them no justice or service? I'll explain it. For example, doctors give placebo pills to patients to soothe their paranoia when they feel that they may be sicker than they are. The placebo pills have no curing or healing agents in them. It's a fake treatment. The placebo pill's sole purpose is to soothe the patient mentally rather than to heal them because theoretically, there's nothing wrong.

Most of the time, patients dramatize their worries about their health, and the doctors conclude there's nothing wrong with them and prescribe them placebo pills to give them hope. It's a psychosomatic fixation. Most importantly, because the patient thinks their getting medicine to restore their health, they miraculously feel better. Now listen, they don't feel better because something was wrong; they start to feel better because their faith was placed in a mindset to believe they will feel better regardless after taking those pills. Their changed perspective mentally cultivated healing, even though nothing was wrong. You see that. It sounds bizarre, but this is very true and happens every day.

Doctors give patients doses of placebo pills because it gives them hope. It gives them faith in something and facilitates them to promote a healing attitude. On the other hand, imagine taking a dose of Jesus on a daily bases; replace them placebo pills with God's word. Every day, you'll get a healthy dose of God's word to heal and cure your ailment. The ailment of self-doubt, unworthiness, inferiority, and every other infirmity known to man.

Imagine having hope and faith in God's word to believe and trust in your heart that you're healed and set free just as The Bible says. Believe that God can and will work it out for you. Have a little faith. God will walk that walk and talk that talk with you. Its time for you to believe it.

Chapter 19
Create Your Environment

When you are on the road to healing, you must make sure your environment is positive and uplifting. You need an atmosphere conducive to healing. The places we chose to dwell in and the people we decide to spend our life with will influence us a lot. That's why it's crucial to preserve an environment and friendships that reflect and promote positive habits, healthy behaviors, and not deplete us or block our progression in our healing or life in general.

Your environment is the incubator for your healing. It keeps your healing safe and covered just as a mother's womb does for her unborn child during pregnancy. There's a process for everything God does in our lives. The method of birth, for example, begins at conception. After conception, the baby grows for nine months inside the mother's womb. When the pregnancy has reached full term, the baby is then ready to be born and meet his or her family, who has long anticipated the baby's arrival.

Our healing is like the birthing process, and we must hold firm to it with endless anticipation. Before we tap into the full manifestation of our healing, we must first conceive it in our minds. Afterward, we impregnate our hearts (the womb) daily with positive healing seeds (God's Word and encouragement). Once we are filled, and our faith has grown unwavering, our full healing is then manifested and birthed into our lives. It's all a process.

However, healing cannot become sufficiently manifested in a wicked and depressing environment. You cannot grow a rose in the darkness. It won't matter how much you water that rose. Without the sun, it won't blossom. We are the rose, and the sun is what we need in our environment to heal and fully bloom. The water correlates to our encouragement, faith, and positive thoughts. It all falls in line, and neither one cannot function without the other. Be sure that the company you keep and your environment is positively influencing your mind and thoughts.

The Company You Keep

The people you allow in your presence regularly, believe it or not, influence your vision considerably. People who are on the same journey as you and are in agreement with your revelation, will facilitate your healing and support your growth. They will always speak life and sustain you during the bad times. They will want to see you shine and flourish and will root for your success - always.

Your friendships and relationships can either bestow life or death to your vision. It's imperative you share and express, only during your healing course, your journey with those you trust to support and lift you. It'll burden you to attempt to flourish within the presence of people who are unconstructive and refuse to vibrate higher. Their habits and ways are no longer your ways and thoughts. Ignoring this will wear you out, and you'll slowly slip into discouragement and deviate from your healing process all because of your environment and company kept.

Often, elevation begets separation. You can always be an example to those around you, and you can always speak life to them as well, but can they do the same is the question? When you are demanding to break a cycle and free yourself from bondage, you cannot do it with any and everybody, especially with those who want to remain bound. You also cannot blossom and grow alongside people who will damage and speak negatively about you and your breakthrough. That's why your environment and the company you keep are essential to the healing process. Not only relating to your healing but as mentioned before, in life in general. Vibrate higher.

What Are You Watching and Listening To?

Let's discuss the content we chose to watch and the music that goes along with it. Did you know that television can sway and contribute to your way of thinking? The music we listen to impacts our moods and emotions too. There are many societal habits developed from what we chose to absorb from television and music. With that being said, music and TV play a significant role in how we think, feel, and respond to situations.

Let's talk about it. Most of our downtime consists of watching television or listening to music. In today's society, if you don't have cable, you're either streaming through a device, tuned into social media, or getting entertainment from internet sites. We also listen to music on our way to work, during workouts, and throughout our emotional high and lows. With TV and music being such a big platform for our visual and listening motivation, it's only right to ensure we are selective in what we consume during our healing course. Be very selective.

Now, I'm not saying that you should eliminate all options concerning what you chose to listen to and watch, I'm not insinuating that at all. Simply put, you should incorporate more inspirational and uplifting content regularly. You cannot heal and be encouraged while listening and watching content that will plant seeds in your heart that is contrary to healing and elevating. Faith comes by hearing, and hearing by the Word of God (Romans 10:17). I also want to let you know that faith-building messages you watch and listen to do not always have to be religious content as well. There are millions of positive words and encouraging materials all over the internet and the world today. With the ease of a few clicks, you can stream and watch life building, and inspirational messages anywhere form all over the world. There are many bloggers out there who place positive content on the internet for free, and not all of them are famous or well known. You can build faith from stimulating messengers from whom you can connect with and speaks to your spirit in a very positive and enriching way.

There are many life coaches, inspirational speakers, mentors, counselors, poets, and writers out here speaking life and elevation to their community. Many musicians don't necessarily make Christian music, but they do craft enriching and inspiring music for their listeners to help you rise above adversaries. As long as the content you digest from TV and music is in line with what God is doing in your life concerning your healing and breakthrough, it'll facilitate your healing to manifest.

<u>**Seeing is Believing**</u>

Last but not least, write down your goals and desires to be healed. It is a proven fact that when aspirations are written down, you are more likely to accomplish them. Regularly write down positive and healing thoughts and reflections along with your faith-building scriptures. Read and feed your soul, positive books, and poetry. Keep an encouraging reaffirming journal. Jot down only enriching things in it. Put pictures and reminders in your diary of the good things that make you happy and the times you were at your most joyful and healthiest. Doing this will prepare your mind and spirit for the healing transformation to take place. The plan is to get your full life back to a pre-painful position before all the damage.

As often as you can, write reaffirming words to yourself, positive messages, you heard that resonated with you down and place them in plain sight in your environment. Whether it be at your desk at work, your bathroom mirror, your car, your nightstand, or any other place, meditate on those visuals often. The more you soak up those life empowering demonstrations, the more healing will attract to you and manifest in your body, mind, and soul. Nothing will stop you or get in your way at that point because you'll be so focused on the process. Most importantly, as I close, I want you to know that you are loved and that no one else approval or opinion matters. Always believe without a shadow of a doubt that you are healed and set free. Continue to call things into existence that do not exist (Romans 4:17). In other words, regardless of what it looks like now, you are calling yourself heald despite the current circumstances.

Chapter 20

Stand Firm in Victory, You are Free

Whomever God sets free, is free indeed (John 8:36). When you chose to rise above your unfavorable circumstances, you decided to operate in the divine purpose inside of you. You decided to be whole. You agreed to position firmly in victory. Stay rooted in this revelation forever—no matter where you are, and no matter what mountain stands before, you can triumph over any hindrance.

I want you to know that God loves you so much and that you do not have to stay complacent in a situation that is contrary to a fulfilling, happy, good life. You were created to lift others. Your story may have started dreadfully; however, God can use your testimony to strengthen and encourage others. No one was able to walk your shoes and survive, but you defied all odds.

You are brave, smart, resourceful, attractive, loving, sophisticated, and every other positive and pleasing thing under the sun. It's all wrapped up and stitched perfectly within your genetic make-up. Don't cry- don't worry. God got you!

Forget about every terrible word spoken to you. Denounce all the bad seeds thrown on your soul to cause you to fail. Leave horrible memories and people in the past that served no enriching purpose in your life. Continue to exercise the healing process in every area of your life. Keep your head held high, because you are an ambassador of Christ. You were once bent but never broken—stand firm in your victory, my friend. You are free and will always remain free, indeed—no more shame and no more bondage.

Dear Heavenly Father, I pray that every compelling word read has been powerfully penetrated within the depths of every reader's soul. I profess power, dominion, and confidence over everyone's life who has chosen to examine this book. I declare your divine and definite purpose reveals itself in their life, dear Lord; therefore, they walk in authority. I pray your unchanging truth is released, and endless joy is manifested in their life right away. Amen.